Simon Peter
Youth Edition

SIMON PETER:
FLAWED BUT FAITHFUL DISCIPLE

Simon Peter: Flawed but Faithful Disciple
978-1-5018-4598-7 Hardcover with jacket
978-1-5018-4599-4 eBook
978-1-5018-4600-7 Large Print

Simon Peter: DVD
978-1-5018-4603-8

Simon Peter: Leader Guide
978-1-5018-4601-4
978-1-5018-4602-1 eBook

Simon Peter: Youth Edition
978-1-5018-4610-6
978-1-5018-4611-3 eBook

Simon Peter: Children's Leader Guide
978-1-5018-4612-0

For more information,
visit www.AdamHamilton.org

Also by Adam Hamilton

24 Hours That Changed the World

Christianity and World Religions

Christianity's Family Tree

Confronting the Controversies

Creed

Enough

Faithful

Final Words from the Cross

Forgiveness

Half Truths

John

Leading Beyond the Walls

Love to Stay

Making Sense of the Bible

Moses

Not a Silent Night

Revival

Seeing Gray in a World of Black and White

Selling Swimsuits in the Arctic

Speaking Well

The Call

The Journey

The Way

Unafraid

Unleashing the Word

When Christians Get It Wrong

Why?

ADAM HAMILTON

Author of *The Call* and *Moses*

SIMON PETER

FLAWED BUT FAITHFUL DISCIPLE

Youth Edition

by Mike Poteet

Abingdon Press / Nashville

CONTENTS

INTRODUCTION

From *Simon Peter*, by Adam Hamilton:

While Simon Peter's shortcomings are clearly on display in the Gospels, so also are his courage, his determination, his longing to follow Jesus even if it costs him his life. The early church knew how his story ended after his dramatic denial of Jesus on the night Jesus was arrested. Following Jesus' resurrection and ascension, Peter would, in fact, become the rock upon which the church was built. He would carry his cross to follow Jesus. He would lay down his life for the gospel. While in Peter's flaws Christians might see themselves, they might also see themselves in the moments of Peter's courage and faithfulness, and ultimately they might see in him a picture of what they might aspire to be when empowered and led by the Spirit.

Adam Hamilton calls Simon Peter the "prince of the apostles." He's the disciple who speaks up boldly and courageously, the one who's mentioned by name far more in the Gospels than any other disciple. Yet he's also the one who gets it wrong, who falters, who misunderstands, who even denies

Jesus. Simon Peter is the one who's most like you and me, and like everyone who seeks to follow Jesus. Simon Peter is the flawed, but ultimately faithful, disciple.

Pastor and author Adam Hamilton explores Simon Peter and the lessons we can learn from him in his book *Simon Peter: Flawed but Faithful Disciple*. The book will be of interest to both adults and young people. With the latter audience in mind, we are offering this youth leader guide.

While this Youth Edition will be used most profitably as part of a church-wide study of Adam Hamilton's book, it can also be used on its own, not only because it includes extensive quotations from Hamilton's book but also because it encourages direct engagement with several texts from the Gospels and the Acts of the Apostles showcasing Simon Peter's strengths and weaknesses as a follower of Jesus—the virtues and vices from which all of us, young and old, can learn.

This study includes the following sessions, each one corresponding to a chapter in Adam Hamilton's book:

Session 1: The Call of the Fisherman

Youth will explore how Jesus' call to discipleship is a gracious "interruption" of our lives, drawing us into an extraordinary relationship with God in the midst of our seemingly ordinary experiences.

Session 2: Walking with Jesus in the Storms

Youth will examine how Jesus' walk with Simon Peter on a stormy sea conveys deep truths about God's presence with us in the midst of life's troubles and challenges, as well as ways in which we can demonstrate bold trust in Jesus' saving presence and power.

Session 3: Bedrock or Stumbling Block?

Youth will consider what it means to profess belief in Jesus as the Son of God. They will ask themselves how much they embrace or reject Jesus' description of his mission, and how far they embody his self-sacrificial service in their own lives.

Session 4: "I Will Not Deny You"

Youth will reflect on Peter's denial of Jesus and confess ways in which they deny Jesus today. They will also give thanks for God's great faithfulness to us even when we prove unfaithful.

Session 5: From Cowardice to Courage

Youth will contemplate the radical change in Peter's life after Easter and explore the role of the Holy Spirit in believers' lives today. They will also talk about and plan ways to actively "feed Jesus' sheep," as he commanded Peter, in their community and in the world.

Session 6: The Rest of the Story

Youth will reflect on Peter's vision in the Book of Acts of God's radically inclusive love and will ask how much their lives and their life together as a youth ministry and a congregation reflect that love.

The sessions are designed for group use, although individuals may read the book and complete many of the activities by themselves with only minor modification.

Each of the six sessions includes opening and closing prayers, at least one Scripture reading, and a wide range of reflection and discussion questions. Choose from the questions and other activities (including, in most sessions, a science experiment or demonstration) as your group's time and interest allow.

May this study give those who read it a deeper appreciation of Simon Peter's journey of discipleship and encouraging insight for their own.

1.

THE CALL OF THE FISHERMAN

Opening Activity: Simon Peter Scavenger Hunt

Supplies: newspapers, magazines

> **From *Simon Peter*, by Adam Hamilton:**
>
> The Gospel writers . . . lift up Simon Peter as representing those of us who believe in and seek to follow Jesus. Like Peter, you and I have chosen to follow Jesus. We've given up something to answer his call. At our best we would, like Peter, boldly proclaim that we would die for Christ if necessary. Yet we've all at times lost our courage, taken our eyes off of Jesus, misunderstood his teaching, and even denied him. Just as Jesus reveals and represents God, Simon Peter represents all who seek to follow Jesus.

Form as many teams of two to four participants as total group size will allow. Give teams five minutes to find pictures of as many of the following as possible in the newspapers and magazines. Each picture found is worth a point; if a group finds a picture of one of the items no other group finds, that picture is worth two points. The team with the most points wins.

fish
fishing
a lake
a boat
a storm
rocks and stones
ghost
keys
church
king
dirty feet
sword
rooster
campfire
sheep
blanket or sheet
Peter
Jesus

All of these items connect, in some way, to the subject of our study, Simon Peter. Depending on how much you already know about Peter and his life, you may "get" many or even all of the connections; if not, you will understand them by the time the study is finished. Either way, you will also gain an appreciation of what Simon Peter still has to teach us about being a disciple of Jesus Christ.

Opening Prayer

After the scavenger hunt, open your discussion with this prayer or one of your own:

Lord Jesus, your holy interruptions in our lives challenge us to leave behind everything that would get in our way as we try to follow you and share your love. May your Spirit help us trust you whenever and however you call us, so we may discover how deep and abundant life can be when we live it trusting you. Amen.

Read and Reflect on Scripture

One day Jesus was standing beside Lake Gennesaret when the crowd pressed in around him to hear God's word. Jesus saw two boats sitting by the lake. The fishermen had gone ashore and were washing their nets. Jesus boarded one of the boats, the one that belonged to Simon, then asked him to row out a little distance from the shore. Jesus sat down and taught the crowds from the boat. When he finished speaking to the crowds, he said to Simon, "Row out farther, into the deep water, and drop your nets for a catch."

Simon replied, "Master, we've worked hard all night and caught nothing. But because you say so, I'll drop the nets."

So they dropped the nets and their catch was so huge that their nets were splitting. They signaled for their partners in the other boat to come and help them. They filled both boats so full that they were about to sink. When Simon Peter saw the catch, he fell at Jesus' knees and said, "Leave me, Lord, for I'm a sinner!" Peter and those with him were overcome with amazement because of the number of fish they caught. James and John, Zebedee's sons, were Simon's partners and they were amazed too.

Jesus said to Simon, "Don't be afraid. From now on, you will be fishing for people." As soon as they brought the boats to the shore, they left everything and followed Jesus.

—Luke 5:1-11

Discuss:

- What, if anything, did you already know about Simon Peter before starting this study? How would you sum up your impressions of him?
- Why do you think Luke doesn't tell us anything about what Jesus preached from Peter's boat that day?

Continue your discussion of Simon Peter's call using the following insights and questions.

From *Simon Peter*, by Adam Hamilton:

But Jesus' strategy was about more than finding the best spot to preach. He wanted to invite Simon Peter's help. . . .

He asks us to give our time, and sometimes to borrow our stuff, in order to accomplish his work. He likes to use our skills, our abilities, whatever is at our disposal that we can offer. But Jesus doesn't always ask for our help in the way he called on Peter.

- What of yours—your skills, abilities, resources—does Jesus want to "borrow" and use to do God's work today? How do you know when Jesus is asking to "borrow your stuff"?

From *Simon Peter*, by Adam Hamilton:

Even though it's Jesus who asks for our help, and even though we seek to be Christ's followers, we will often feel reluctant and hesitant. We make excuses. . . . But Peter didn't. . . He simply got in the boat. There's a lesson in that for us.

- What are some excuses you've made when Jesus has asked you to do something?
- What things have you done with reluctance, and only because Jesus asked you to (see verse 5)? What happened as a result?
- What advice would you give to another Christian who is feeling reluctant to do something they believe (or even strongly suspect) Jesus is asking her or him to do?
- Why does Simon Peter respond to the miraculous catch of fish as he does (see verse 6)?
- When, if ever, have you responded to God's presence in fear? What happened? How, if at all, did you hear Jesus telling you, "Don't be afraid" (verse 10)?
- When, if ever, have you felt afraid as a result of following Jesus? What happened? Would you repeat what you did? Why or why not?

- What does Jesus mean when he says Simon Peter will be "fishing for people" (verse 10)? How do Jesus' followers "fish for people" today? How do you?
- Simon Peter, James, and John "left everything and followed Jesus" (verse 11). What have you left behind, literally or otherwise, to follow Jesus?
- Adam Hamilton sees Simon Peter as a flawed follower. Think about one of your flaws as a follower of Jesus. How do you (or how could you) talk about that flaw with other people in a way that draws attention to Jesus' continued faithfulness to you?

Game: Interrupting Inquisition[1]

From *Simon Peter*, by Adam Hamilton:
Jesus routinely inconveniences his followers.

Recruit two self-confident volunteers to stand in front of the whole group. One is the Storyteller. He or she has five minutes to tell a story (fable, Bible story, plot of a movie, something done for summer vacation…almost any narrative will do). The Storyteller must speak in short, complete sentences—no run-on sentences or "uhs" and "ums."

The other volunteer is the Questioner. Her or his goal is to keep the Storyteller from finishing the story in the allowed time by interrupting with as many relevant questions as possible.

The Questioner must wait until the Storyteller pauses and may only ask questions that follow from what the Storyteller has just said—no completely "out of left field" questions, but funny and creative, even silly, questions are encouraged. Yes-No questions are not allowed.

The Storyteller cannot ignore any question, but must answer them all. "I don't know" is not an acceptable answer. Made-up answers are allowed and encouraged. The Storyteller may not end the story prematurely.

For example, this Storyteller is talking about the first Christmas:

Storyteller: Mary and Joseph had to go to Bethlehem.
Questioner: Where is Bethlehem?
Storyteller: In Israel. When they got there, they stayed in a stable.
Questioner: What's a stable?

14

Storyteller: A barn for animals.

Questioner: How many zebras were in the stable?

…and so on.

Discuss:

- How do you feel when you are interrupted in real life?
- Have you ever been glad to be interrupted? What happened?
- When do you believe Jesus has inconvenienced or interrupted you? How did you respond?
- When, if ever, does following Jesus mean inconveniencing or interrupting other people?
- How and why does Jesus need to interrupt you today?

Science Experiment: In Deep and Under Pressure![2]

What You Need

empty, unlabeled 2-liter plastic bottle with twist-on cap
ruler
permanent ink marker
sharp nail
masking tape or duct tape
water
shallow square or rectangular bin

What You'll Do

1. Measure three inches up from the bottle's bottom and mark the spot with the ink marker.
2. Measure five inches straight up from your first mark and mark the spot.
3. Use the nail to carefully poke small holes in the bottle at each of your marked spots.
4. Put tape over each hole.
5. Fill the bottle completely with water and twist the bottle's cap on tightly.
6. Place the bottle upright in the bin.

7. Pull off the two pieces of tape and watch the water as it pours into the bin.

You'll watch water flow out of the bottle faster and more forcefully from the lower hole than the higher one. The deeper the water is in the bottle, the more pressure it is under.

For Reflection

- When has being under pressure forced you to go faster and more forcefully?
- How, if at all, did God use that experience to help you grow as a person? as a Christian?
- Do you think God deliberately puts us under pressure so we can grow in faith? Why or why not?

Song Suggestion

From *Simon Peter,* by Adam Hamilton:

If you are a Christian, you are a part of this movement. Have you ever stopped to think about what that word implies? It suggests something that is always moving, not sitting still—always reaching out in love, always fishing for people. Are you sitting still and asking God to use someone else, or are you part of a movement?

Sing or read aloud together "The Summons" (*The Faith We Sing*, 2130),* a song all about answering the call of Christ.

Discuss:

- Which of the things that Jesus asks us to do in this song excites, frightens, or intrigues you the most? Why?
- How are you a different person because of a time when you heard Jesus call your name? How are you reaching out in love to others because of Jesus?

*See John Bell, 1987, "The Summons," *The Faith We Sing*, Pew Edition (Nashville: Abingdon Press, 2000), 2130.

Bible Extra: Isaiah 6:1-8

From *Simon Peter,* by Adam Hamilton:

The first part of Jesus' call was simply not to be fearful. Have you ever noticed how many times *that* message occurs in the Gospels?

Peter is not the only person in Scripture who experiences awe and fear as a first reaction to a heavenly call. So does the prophet Isaiah, who lived some seven hundred years before Christ:

In the year of King Uzziah's death, I saw the Lord sitting on a high and exalted throne, the edges of his robe filling the temple. Winged creatures were stationed around him. Each had six wings: with two they veiled their faces, with two their feet, and with two they flew about. They shouted to each other, saying:

"Holy, holy, holy is the Lord of heavenly forces!
All the earth is filled with God's glory!"

The doorframe shook at the sound of their shouting, and the house was filled with smoke.

I said, "Mourn for me; I'm ruined! I'm a man with unclean lips, and I live among a people with unclean lips. Yet I've seen the king, the Lord of heavenly forces!"

Then one of the winged creatures flew to me, holding a glowing coal that he had taken from the altar with tongs. He touched my mouth and said, "See, this has touched your lips. Your guilt has departed, and your sin is removed."

Then I heard the Lord's voice saying, "Whom should I send, and who will go for us?"

I said, "I'm here; send me."

—Isaiah 6:1-8

Discuss:

- How is Isaiah's reaction to being in God's presence like and unlike Simon Peter's reaction to being in Jesus' presence after the miraculous catch of fish?
- How do Isaiah's and Simon Peter's experiences prepare each man for carrying out a divinely given mission?
- When, if ever, have you told God to send you? What happened as a result?

Optional Extension: Illustrate Isaiah's vision, drawing your own images or creating a collage of pictures from magazines and newspapers.

Closing Questions

Wrap up your session by discussing the following questions:

- What is one new insight or question you have after today's session about how Jesus calls us to be his disciples?
- What is one way you will actively be a "fisher for people" this week?

Closing Prayer

Use this prayer or one of your own:

Faithful God, thank you for the call your Son, Jesus, extends to share your love with others. By your Spirit, may we trust his strength and grace enough to respond obediently, knowing that no matter the depths into which he calls us to go, he has already gone ahead of us to prepare blessings. Amen.

2.

WALKING WITH JESUS
IN THE STORMS

Opening Activity: Christen Your Boat

Supplies: one sheet of 8½-by-11 paper per participant, pens or pencils

Optional: large plastic tub filled with water

> ### From *Simon Peter,* by Adam Hamilton:
> I think this is what the Gospel writers hoped their readers would understand when they included the story of Jesus walking on the water, not only that he once did what only God can do but also that he continues to come to us in the storms of life, climbs into our boat, and rides out the storm with us.

Make sure each person has a sheet of paper. Instruct them to fold the piece of paper into a boat, using simple instructions such as those at https://www.wikihow.com/Make-a-Paper-Boat. When participants have folded their boats, invite them to "christen" the boats by writing a name on the boat. Invite volunteers to talk about why they gave their boats the names they did.

Optional: Float the boats in a large plastic tub (or other container) filled with water.

This session's Scripture reading features Jesus getting into a boat, as the first session's reading did. But it is also a story about Peter getting out of a boat—a model for us of stepping outside our comfort zones in faith to be a part of what Jesus is doing.

Opening Prayer

Use this prayer or one of your own:

God of power and wisdom, who rules surging waters and walks the waves of the sea: In this time of listening and learning, quiet all the storms that threaten to draw our attention away from you; and, by your Spirit, help us to recognize more clearly your Son, our Savior, Jesus Christ. Amen.

Read and Reflect on Scripture

This session's Scripture passage takes place just after Jesus has miraculously fed a large crowd of people—"about five thousand men plus women and children" (Matthew 14:21)—with only five loaves of bread and two fish. (That miracle is, apart from Jesus' resurrection, the only miracle recorded in all four Gospels.)

Right then, Jesus made the disciples get into the boat and go ahead to the other side of the lake while he dismissed the crowds. When he sent them away, he went up onto a mountain by himself to pray. Evening came and he was alone. Meanwhile, the boat, fighting a strong headwind, was being battered by the waves and was already far away from land. Very early in the morning he came to his disciples, walking on the lake. When the disciples saw him walking on the lake, they were terrified and said, "It's a ghost!" They were so frightened they screamed.

Just then Jesus spoke to them, "Be encouraged! It's me. Don't be afraid."

Peter replied, "Lord, if it's you, order me to come to you on the water."

And Jesus said, "Come."

Then Peter got out of the boat and was walking on the water toward Jesus. But when Peter saw the strong wind, he became frightened. As he began to sink, he shouted, "Lord, rescue me!"

Jesus immediately reached out and grabbed him, saying, "You man of weak faith! Why did you begin to have doubts?" When they got into the boat, the wind settled down.

Then those in the boat worshipped Jesus and said, "You must be God's Son!"

—*Matthew 14:22-33*

Option: For an active and creative Scripture reading, recruit volunteers to pantomime the roles of Jesus, Peter, and the disciples as one or more other volunteers read aloud. Act out the disciples' motions in and reactions to the storm, their terror when they first see Jesus, Jesus and Peter's walk on the water, and the disciples' worship of Jesus as the storm dies down.

Discuss:

- How do you imagine you would have reacted if you had seen Jesus walking toward you on the lake in the middle of the storm in this story?
- Jesus called to his disciples in the boat, "It's me" (verse 27). As Adam Hamilton points out, Matthew's original Greek text literally translates, "I am." What might Jesus' way of talking about himself have meant to devout Jews like his disciples, who knew the story of Moses hearing God's Name (read it in Exodus 3:13-15)? How might the story in Exodus help us understand the disciples' worship of Jesus at this story's end?

Continue your discussion of Simon Peter's call using the following insights and questions.

From *Simon Peter*, by Adam Hamilton:

When we're walking through the storms that inevitably we will face, we should remember these stories of Jesus coming to the disciples on the sea. We can remember his words to them: "Be encouraged! It's me. Don't be afraid." Those three little words—don't be afraid—are the most frequently spoken words from God to human beings in Scripture. You'll find that phrase more than 140 times in your Bible.

- Why do you think God's message to us is so frequently, "Don't be afraid"?
- How have you heard other people finish the sentence, "Lord, if it's you . . ." (Matthew 14:28)? How, if ever, have you asked Jesus to show or prove his identity—and how, if at all, do you believe he has responded?
- Adam Hamilton writes Peter's request to walk out to Jesus on the water "sounds almost idiotic." Do you agree? Why or why not? What motivates Peter at this point, do you think?
- Why do you think Peter begins to sink: because he feels "frightened" (verse 30), because he has "doubts" (verse 31), or because of something else? How are fear and doubt alike and different?
- Adam Hamilton imagines Jesus asking Peter, "Why did you look away?" When, in your life, do you look away from Jesus? What happens when you do? How, specifically, do you refocus your attention on him?
- Do you think doubts always indicate "weak faith" (verse 31), as Jesus describes Peter's faith in that moment? Why or why not? How should Christians react when they experience doubts?

From *Simon Peter*, by Adam Hamilton:

This was the first time in the Gospels that the disciples declared Jesus to be God's Son, the first time they declared this kind of faith in him. They had known him as a carpenter from Nazareth. They knew him as a rabbi who called them to be fishers of people. They had seen him perform some miracles. Though the disciples didn't yet understand the

affirmations the church would one day make about him—
that Jesus was "fully God" and "fully human," that he was God
the Son in human flesh—they had nevertheless experienced
God's presence in this man that night on the sea.

- Why do you think this story immediately follows the story of Jesus
miraculously feeding the hungry crowd? What do these two stories,
when read together, tell us about Jesus that either story, by itself,
might not?
- What does the title "Son of God" mean for you? Is it one you use to
talk and think about and pray to Jesus? Why or why not?

Identifying Our Storms

Supplies: magazines and newspapers, markers, glue/tape, posterboard

Optional: computer with Internet access and printer

From *Simon Peter*, by Adam Hamilton:

During the storms in our lives, when the waves are crashing
up against our boat and we fear we won't survive, Jesus still
walks on the water to wherever we are. He gets in the boat
with us. Jesus may not make the storm go away, as he did
for Peter and the disciples. . . . But Jesus is riding it out with
us, and somehow that makes the storm less terrifying. That
is part of what the Christian's spiritual life is about. Feeling
Jesus' presence with us enables us to be calmed, even if the
storm is raging all around us.

Discuss:

- What's the most terrifying storm you've ever seen or been caught
in? How did you handle your fear during the storm?

Look through magazines and newspapers for images and words picturing
and describing storms. (If possible, search for and print out storm images
from the Internet too.) Work together with others to create a collage of these
images. Leave some space in between images.

Discuss:

- What situations in your life have you faced, or are you currently facing, that you would describe as "tempestuous storms"? Why?
- How have you experienced Jesus' presence with you "in your boat" during these storms? How has his presence made the storms you face "less terrifying"?
- How might Jesus be present through you with other people who are facing storms in their lives?

Using markers, fill in the spaces in the collage with words or sketches answering the discussion questions. Display the finished collage where others in your congregation can see it.

Science Experiment: How Strong are the Bonds?[3]

Supplies: See "What You'll Need," below.

From *Simon Peter*, by Adam Hamilton:

After Peter stepped out of the boat, he actually walked on water! But then, as Matthew tells us, Peter noticed the strong wind, and it frightened him. When he became frightened, he began to sink. He cried out, "Lord, rescue me!" And Jesus immediately reached out his hand and lifted Peter up. . . .

After rescuing him, Jesus said to Peter, "You man of weak faith! Why did you begin to have doubts?" The Gospel doesn't tell us anything about Jesus' tone of voice or inflection. But I don't think he was really chastising Peter. After all, Peter showed more faith than the eleven who remained in the boat. . . . I imagine Jesus meaning something like: "Peter, why did you look away? I had you. You didn't need to worry! If you had only trusted me."

Perform this science experiment to illustrate the importance of having a strong connection to Christ.

What You'll Need

two identical clear, tall drinking glasses
water
liquid dish soap
spoon
two pieces of scrap paper, approximately the same size

What You'll Do

1. Fill the two glasses with water to the same level.
2. Add and stir some dish soap into one of the glasses. (Start with about 6 teaspoons. You can repeat this experiment several times and see what differences, if any, you observe using different amounts of dish soap.)
3. Crumple each piece of scrap paper into a small, tight ball. Make the balls as equal in size as you can.
4. Slowly put one paper ball in each glass.
5. Observe what happens to the paper ball in the glass with the water and dish soap.

Dish soap weakens the hydrogen bonds in water (chemical formula H_2O, remember?). Weaker bonds mean lower surface tension—the "phenomenon in which the surface of a liquid, where the liquid is in contact with gas, acts like a thin elastic sheet."[4] Lower surface tension means the paper ball can't stay on top of the water.

For Reflection

*   Surface tension can't explain Jesus walking on water (surface tension is never that strong, after all!), but Peter did only start to sink when he "weakened his bond" with Jesus by focusing on the storm instead of the Son of God. What has threatened (or still threatens) to draw your attention away from Jesus, "weakening your bond" with him? What happens in those moments?
*   What does the time Jesus spent in prayer before he walked on the water suggest about how we can strengthen our bond with God?
*   Do you believe we can weaken our bond with Jesus and God so badly it breaks? Why or why not?

Be Part of Something Unbelievable

Supplies: None needed

From *Simon Peter,* by Adam Hamilton:

Peter didn't just call to Jesus and step out of the boat. He waited for Jesus to bid him to step out of the boat and come to him. He did not trust in his own ability to walk on the water. But he trusted that if Jesus called him to do it, he could.

Jesus said, "Come!" And Peter stepped out of the boat. Can you imagine that? Peter had been working on the water for his entire adult life. His experience had taught him that getting out of a boat on the lake meant that a person either would have to sink or swim; walking was not an option. And in a storm like that, and being far from shore, swimming wasn't much of an option either. Yet here was Simon Peter, stepping out of the boat, no life jacket, no life buoy. Just Jesus.

Adam Hamilton offers several examples of people he knows who are answering Jesus' call to get out of their "boats," from a senior citizen who donated blood for the first time to members of his congregation involved in prison ministries. "When we are motivated primarily by faith rather than fear," he writes, "we recognize, as Peter did, that the adventure is *outside the boat.*"

Discuss:

- What opportunities for joining Jesus in an "adventure . . . *outside the boat*" exist in your congregation and community?
- How do you decide which of these opportunities Jesus is calling you to take advantage of?
- What chances to be a part of the unbelievable things God is doing in the world today do you see that others don't already see? What are you doing about those?

Music Activity: "Precious Lord, Take My Hand"

Supplies: hymnals

Sing or read aloud together "Precious Lord, Take My Hand" (*The United Methodist Hymnal*, 474).* You can also listen to and watch several artists' recordings of this song online.

Adam Hamilton connects this song to the story of Jesus and Peter on the water: "When he wrote this hymn, Thomas Dorsey was sinking, and the only one who might rescue him from his inconsolable grief [about the death of his wife, Nettie] was the one who took Simon Peter's hand."

For Reflection:

- When do you feel (or when have you felt) tired, weak, and worn, as in this song's lyrics?
- If you pray to God when you feel those feelings, how do you pray? If you don't, why not?
- **Optional:** Read more about composer Thomas Dorsey's faith and work in gospel music at the PBS webpage "This Far By Faith: Thomas Dorsey" (https://www.pbs.org/thisfarbyfaith/people /thomas_dorsey.html).

Closing Questions

Wrap up your session by discussing the following questions:

- Adam Hamilton writes that part of Peter's role is to help us understand who Jesus is. How, in the "story" of your life, do you try to help other people understand who Jesus is?
- What is one new insight or question you have about who Jesus is as a result of today's session?
- What is one action you will take this week in response to today's session?

---

*See Thomas Dorsey, 1932, "Precious Lord, Take My Hand," *The United Methodist Hymnal* (Nashville: The United Methodist Publishing House, 1989), 474.

Closing Prayer

Use this prayer or one of your own:

Jesus Christ, Son of God: You call us to follow you even when storms roar around us and we are frightened enough to scream. By your Spirit, make us courageous enough to get out of where we are most comfortable. Strengthen us to walk with you even when it makes us uncertain, trusting that being with you is the right place to be, and that you will never let us sink so deep your power and love cannot save us. Amen.

3.

BEDROCK OR STUMBLING BLOCK?

Opening Activity: Famous Nicknames

Supplies: index cards, large sheets of paper, or markerboard, markers

> **From *Simon Peter*, by Adam Hamilton:**
> "Who do you say that I am?" . . .
>
> Up to this point, Jesus has not identified himself as the Messiah. The disciples had watched him heal the sick, cast out demons, feed the multitudes, calm the wind and the waves of the sea, even walk on water. But he had never come right out and said he was the Messiah. And they had never come right out and asked. But Jesus brought them here, to this place, to ask them this question. And who was the only disciple courageous, brash, or foolish enough to attempt an answer? Simon Peter.

Write several famous nicknames on index cards—of famous people (real or fictional), of well-known places, of historic events—that group members are likely to recognize, one nickname per card. As youth arrive, offer each one the chance to draw a card (without looking, of course) from your "deck" of index cards. Have participants sketch clues on large sheets of paper or a markerboard so that others can guess the nickname they selected. A guess is only counted correct if the nickname is given. (For example, "Superman" would be incorrect, but "Man of Steel" would be correct; "Chicago" would be incorrect, but "The Windy City" would be correct.)

Tell participants today's session has a lot to do with arguably the most famous nickname in Christian history.

Opening Prayer

Use this prayer or one of your own:

Loving God, you know and call us as you do the stars in heaven: each one by name. Use this time we offer you to illuminate us with true knowledge of your Son—Jesus the Christ. By your Spirit, help us shine as those who humbly and faithfully proclaim him by giving our lives to serve others for his sake and in his name. Amen.

Read and Reflect on Scripture

This session's Scripture passage takes place near Caesarea Philippi, an ancient Roman city in what is today the area of Banias in the Golan Heights. Adam Hamilton provides some background about the location.

From *Simon Peter*, by Adam Hamilton:

Caesarea Philippi was in a predominantly non-Jewish area long associated with the worship of pagan deities. . . .

For centuries, Caesarea Philippi was not a city, but a place of pagan worship known as Panias (or Paneas). Pan, the Greek god of nature, flocks, and the wild, with the torso of a man and hind quarters of a goat, was worshiped at places of great natural beauty. . . .

By the time Jesus brought his disciples here, a temple had been built in front of the cave, and others beside it, the foundations of which can still be seen. One of these temples is believed to be the one built by King Herod the Great in 20 BC and dedicated to Augustus Caesar.

Keep this physical setting in mind as you read the Scriptures in this session.

Now when Jesus came to the area of Caesarea Philippi, he asked his disciples, "Who do people say the Human One is?"

They replied, "Some say John the Baptist, others Elijah, and still others Jeremiah or one of the other prophets."

He said, "And what about you? Who do you say that I am?"

Simon Peter said, "You are the Christ, the Son of the living God."

Then Jesus replied, "Happy are you, Simon son of Jonah, because no human has shown this to you. Rather my Father who is in heaven has shown you. I tell you that you are Peter. And I'll build my church on this rock. The gates of the underworld won't be able to stand against it. I'll give you the keys of the kingdom of heaven. Anything you fasten on earth will be fastened in heaven. Anything you loosen on earth will be loosened in heaven." Then he ordered the disciples not to tell anybody that he was the Christ.

From that time Jesus began to show his disciples that he had to go to Jerusalem and suffer many things from the elders, chief priests, and legal experts, and that he had to be killed and raised on the third day. Then Peter took hold of Jesus and, scolding him, began to correct him: "God forbid, Lord! This won't happen to you." But he turned to Peter and said, "Get behind me, Satan. You are a stone that could make me stumble, for you are not thinking God's thoughts but human thoughts."

Then Jesus said to his disciples, "All who want to come after me must say no to themselves, take up their cross, and follow me. All who want to save their lives will lose them. But all who lose their lives because of me will find them."

—*Matthew 16:13-25*

31

Discuss:

- Why does it matter that Jesus asks his disciples to talk about who he is in a setting like Caesarea Philippi, long associated with pagan gods and named (in Jesus' time) in honor of the Roman Emperor, who was regarded as divine?
- Why do you think Jesus first asks his disciples what other people are saying about him?

Why would people think Jesus might be John the Baptist, Elijah, Jeremiah, or another prophet? Read these Scriptures (and, if available, consult a good Bible dictionary) to find out more about these people:

- John the Baptist: Luke 3:7-20
- Elijah: 1 Kings 17; 2 Kings 2:1-12
- Jeremiah: Jeremiah 7:1-7; 31:31-34

Use the following insights and questions to continue your discussion of the Scripture passage.

From *Simon Peter*, by Adam Hamilton:

Have you ever been somewhere, in a classroom, at the office, or among friends, where someone asks a question, and you are pretty sure you know the answer, but you are not 100 percent sure, and you don't want to look foolish or stupid, so you remain quiet? I have. And that's how I picture what happened there by the Hermon Stream, in the shadow of the temples to Pan and Caesar, with the sheer exposed rock face of Mount Hermon above the disciples. I can see them looking down in silence, not willing to risk giving the wrong answer and not wanting to demonstrate that they are not entirely sure.

- How easy or difficult do you find it to talk about who you believe Jesus is? Are you ever worried or afraid you might say the wrong things about him? Why or why not?
- Jesus says Simon Peter's declaration about him comes directly from God, not human knowledge or understanding (Matthew 16:17).

How does (or how should) this truth influence the way we think about God and Jesus, and how we talk about them to other people?

From *Simon Peter,* by Adam Hamilton:

Binding and loosing were terms applied to the leading rabbis when they debated the law and how to interpret and apply it. What they forbade was bound; what they permitted was loosened. With this statement, Jesus was giving Peter—and, through him, the church—authority to interpret Scripture and to practice church discipline.

- In Matthew 18:18, Jesus gives the authority to bind and loose to all the disciples. In your experience, how helpful or important do you find the church's teaching in understanding the Bible? Why? What do you understand "church discipline" to be? Is it organizing the church's life together, instructing church members who need correction, or something else?
- How well do you think the church remembers it belongs to Christ? When have you experienced the church remembering or forgetting this truth, and how did you respond?
- Jesus promises Peter the "gates of the underworld"—a figure of speech for all forces opposed to God's good will for life—"won't be able to stand against" his church (16:18). How seriously does the church take this promise, in your opinion? How does your congregation show it trusts Jesus' promise—or what more do you think it could be doing? How will you share your thoughts and ideas with your church's leaders?
- Why does Jesus command his disciples not to talk about his identity as the Messiah (verse 20)?
- Read about when Satan tempted Jesus in the wilderness (Matthew 4:1-11; compare Luke 4:1-13). What do you think Jesus hears in Peter's rebuke of him (Matthew 16:22) that makes him call his disciple "Satan" (verse 23)? How does Peter's outburst represent another temptation for Jesus? How does Jesus deal with this temptation?
- When was a time you have denied yourself in order to faithfully follow Jesus?

Knowing the Names of Jesus

Optional Supplies: Bible dictionaries, concordances, pens, and paper

From *Simon Peter*, by Adam Hamilton:

Peter's response to Jesus' question was something of a rebuke to the claims of the emperor. Jesus, he was declaring, wasn't merely *a* son of a dead god, as Augustus Caesar was. He was *the* Son of the living God.

Christians continue to join Simon Peter in this statement of faith. I wake up every morning and yield my life to Jesus once more, hailing him my Christ, my King. What I know about God is largely due to what I've seen, heard, and learned about Jesus. He is, in Paul's words, "the image of the invisible God" (Colossians 1:15), or as the Gospel of John describes him, he is God's word wrapped in human flesh. In John, Jesus says it this way, "If you've seen me, you've seen the Father." (See John 14:9.)

We can't understand this Bible story unless we understand the many names and titles for Jesus in it. Look up each of the following names or titles using the suggested Scripture references (and, if available, a good Bible dictionary or concordance) and, where included, commentary from Adam Hamilton. Write a few words or phrases summarizing what you find out about each one.

Jesus: the Greek form of the Hebrew name Yeshua (Joshua), Matthew 1:21

The Human One (Son of Man): Matthew 16:13, see also Daniel 7:13-14 which describes "one like a human being."

The Messiah (Christ): means "anointed one." Keeping this information and the above quotation from Adam Hamilton in mind, read Isaiah 61:1-4, which describes one of God's servants who receives a different kind of anointing.

Son of the Living God: Keeping in mind Hamilton's words about the Son of God, read Psalm 2.

Discuss:

- What does each of these names and titles tell us about Jesus by itself?
- What do they tell us about Jesus when considered together?
- Adam Hamilton notes that Peter's statement, important as it is, "doesn't represent everything Christians eventually came to believe about Jesus in light of his death and resurrection." We also understand Jesus as our friend; as the Word made flesh; as the atoning sacrifice for sin; as the Savior of the world. What other names and titles for Jesus do you personally find meaningful, and why?

Science Experiment: Reliable Bedrock?[5]

Supplies: See "What You'll Need," below.

From *Simon Peter*, by Adam Hamilton:

Three years later, it was his own disciple, the man who would be the rock upon whom he would build his church, who was encouraging Jesus to pursue the crown without the cross. Peter wasn't intending to lead Jesus astray; he was only using human logic and seeking to look out for his friend. Which reminds me that even our Christian friends, pastors, and counselors can at times lead us away from God's path. They would, like Peter, do it unwittingly, but with real consequences. And we might be Peter for someone else, leading them astray without intending to do so. When we're thinking only human thoughts, we'll often counsel against the hard path, the way of suffering.

What You'll Need

eight-ounce clear plastic cup
thin sponge or scouring pad
granulated sugar
sand (check local arts and crafts stores)
scissors

small length of PVC pipe or a sheet of notebook or copy paper

shallow plastic bin

water

What You'll Do

1. Cut a small, thumb-sized hole in the middle of the cup's bottom.
2. Put the sponge or scouring pad in the cup's bottom, covering the hole.
3. Put a tube into the center of the cup. You can use your length of PVC pipe, or you can simply roll the sheet of paper into a tube. The tube should be about the cup's height and half its diameter.
4. Holding the tube in place with one hand, use the other hand to pour sand around the tube.
5. Pour sugar into the top of the tube.
6. Gently lift the tube out of the cup. You should now have an area of sugar in the middle of the sand.
7. Cover the central area of sugar with a thin layer of sand.
8. Fill the shallow plastic bin with water.
9. Place the cup into the water.

What happens? You've created a sinkhole in your cup because the water dissolves the sugar. The sugar represents limestone underground being dissolved by water, resulting in a collapse of more solid bedrock.

In this session's Scripture passage, Jesus gives Simon the name Peter, or "Rock," because Peter, with his strong confession of faith in him, is the "bedrock" on which Jesus will build the church. But almost immediately afterward, Peter, the church's supposed bedrock, "caves" as much as the sugar in your cup caused the sand to cave, urging Jesus to give up on the self-sacrificial mission God has appointed.

Discuss:

- Describe a time you felt like a "rock" in your faith. Now describe a time you felt like you collapsed in your faith. What prompted these feelings, and what did you do as a result in each case?
- Whom do you admire (whether you know them personally or not) as being "rock-like" in their faith—a committed and confident follower of Christ?

- Why is this session's story about Peter an important one to remember as we think about people, including ourselves, who may be "rock-like" or like collapsing bedrock in faith?

Craft: Nail Cross[6]

Supplies: See "What You'll Need," below.

> ### From *Simon Peter*, by Adam Hamilton:
>
> In response to Peter, Jesus explained that earthly power and glory were not on the path that he was taking—which meant that anyone who was sincere about following him would have to follow a road that would likely take them through suffering as well. He told the disciples plainly: "All who want to come after me must say no to themselves, take up their cross, and follow me" (Matthew 16:24).
>
> The challenge is that we prefer self-fulfillment to self-denial. We would prefer to avoid sacrifice, and instead to play it safe without suffering or personal cost. And we're happy to follow Jesus provided it means blessings and bliss, hope and love, forgiveness and mercy. We want our religion to bless us, but we'd prefer it not ask anything too hard of us in return. This is true for me. I don't like self-denial; I'd prefer to have a convenient faith that doesn't demand too much sacrifice on my part.

What You'll Need

> four steel cut flooring nails, all the same length
> glue dots
> two-foot length of hemp cord or jewelry wire

What You'll Do

1. Place two of the nails side by side, their heads opposite each other, and secure using glue dots.
2. Repeat step 1 with the other pair of nails.

3. Form the shape of a cross by placing and securing one pair of nails on top of the other.
4. Wrap the hemp cord or jewelry wire around the intersection of the nails several times, forming an "X." Tie off the back in a knot.

Discuss:

- Given that, in the ancient Roman Empire, the cross was only a symbol of a terrible punishment reserved for the lowest criminals, how would Jesus' first disciples likely have reacted to what he says in Matthew 16:24?
- How would you put Jesus' words in language people today would easily understand?
- How is Jesus' way of willing self-denial and self-sacrifice different from what people mean when they say about the difficulties they face, "I guess it's my cross to bear"?
- When have you found following Jesus to be hard and inconvenient? How have you responded in these moments?

Closing Questions

Wrap up your session by discussing the following questions:

- What is one new insight or question you have about what following Jesus means as a result of today's session?
- What is one action you will take this week in response to today's session?

Closing Prayer

Use one of your own prayers or the Wesley Covenant Prayer quoted by Adam Hamilton:

I am no longer my own, but yours.
Put me to what you will, rank me with whom you will.
Put me to doing, put me to suffering.
Let me be employed by you or laid aside for you.
Exalted for you or brought low for you.
Let me be full, let me be empty.
Let me have all things, let me have nothing.
I freely and wholeheartedly yield all things to your pleasure and disposal.[7]

4.

"I WILL NOT DENY YOU"

Opening Activity: I Recognize You!

Supplies: scrap paper, pens or pencils, small candies or pennies (three per participant), bucket or other container

From *Simon Peter*, by Adam Hamilton:

Once again, it was Peter, the Rock, who spoke up first and most forcefully. I love how Matthew records his words. In essence he says, "Even if these others abandon you, I will never do that, ever." Bold words from the man who would deny Jesus three times before the night was out. I believe Peter sincerely meant what he said. But when it came down to the moment when he himself might be arrested, he was overcome by fear. Bold and courageous, fearful and flawed. That was Peter.

As participants arrive, give each three small candies or pennies, and have each write a short true or false statement about themselves and their name on a piece of scrap paper. Participants should not tell anyone what they have written.

The leader gathers the statements and reads them aloud, one after the other, without interruption or comment from the group. Then the leader invites volunteers to guess which group member wrote which statement. Each guess costs one candy or penny, so each participant may make three guesses. They may choose to guess the authors of up to three different statements. If they make a successful guess, they keep their candy or penny; if not, it goes into a bucket or other container.

Option: Collect statements from participants before the session via e-mail or text, and write them on newsprint or markerboard for the group's easy reference.

After the game, ask:

- How were you able to recognize who wrote which statements?
- What did you think or feel when someone recognized your statement?

Tell participants that today's session is about how Simon Peter reacted when others recognized him as one of Jesus' followers.

Opening Prayer

Use this prayer or one of your own:

Eternal God, you are faithful to us even when we are unfaithful to you. Only because of your faithfulness, we dare to ask your Spirit's presence as we study the Scripture and seek your Word. May we recognize our own faithfulness and failings in the experiences of Simon Peter, so we may grow as followers of the one he followed, your Son, our Savior, Jesus. Amen.

Read and Reflect on Scripture

This session's first main Bible reading occurs just after Jesus has celebrated the Passover seder with his disciples on the night before his crucifixion.

In the seder (SAY-der) meal, Jews remember how God delivered the Hebrew slaves from Egypt in the Exodus and established a covenant—

a special, binding relationship—with them. According to Matthew, Jesus used bread and wine during the last seder he shared with his disciples to speak of his own body and "blood of the covenant . . . poured out for many so that their sins may be forgiven" (26:28).

> Then Jesus said to his disciples, "Tonight you will all fall away because of me. This is because it is written, *I will hit the shepherd, and the sheep of the flock will go off in all directions.* But after I'm raised up, I'll go before you to Galilee."
>
> Peter replied, "If everyone else stumbles because of you, I'll never stumble."
>
> Jesus said to him, "I assure you that, before the rooster crows tonight, you will deny me three times."
>
> Peter said, "Even if I must die alongside you, I won't deny you." All the disciples said the same thing.
>
> —*Matthew 26:31-35*

In this session's second main Bible reading, we read how Jesus' prediction of Peter's denial came true. Judas betrayed Jesus to armed guards sent by the religious leadership, who took him to the high priest, Caiaphas. Matthew tells us Peter "followed him from a distance" and waited in Caiaphas's courtyard during Jesus' trial (26:58). As Adam Hamilton points out, while Jesus faced his trial, "Peter was about to face his own kind of trial."

> Meanwhile, Peter was sitting outside in the courtyard. A servant woman came and said to him, "You were also with Jesus the Galilean."
>
> But he denied it in front of all of them, saying, "I don't know what you are talking about."
>
> When he went over to the gate, another woman saw him and said to those who were there, "This man was with Jesus, the man from Nazareth."
>
> With a solemn pledge, he denied it again, saying, "I don't know the man."

A short time later those standing there came and said to Peter, "You must be one of them. The way you talk gives you away."

Then he cursed and swore, "I don't know the man!" At that very moment the rooster crowed. Peter remembered Jesus' words, "Before the rooster crows you will deny me three times." And Peter went out and cried uncontrollably.

—*Matthew 26:69-75*

Discuss:

- What significance do you see in the fact that Jesus spoke about his own death's meaning during the Passover seder with his disciples?

Matthew records Jesus quoting Zechariah 13:7 as he foretells his disciples' desertion (Matthew 26:31). Read Zechariah 13. Through the prophet (who was probably active about five hundred years before Jesus), God is announcing a day of judgment against false prophets who mislead God's people into idolatry.

- Why do you think Jesus remembered this Scripture when thinking about how his disciples would abandon him? In Zechariah 13, what does God promise will happen to the portion of God's people left after the judgment?
- What other connections, if any, can you make between this Scripture passage and Jesus' situation?
- Talk about a time you intended to stand by and stand up for someone else no matter what. Did you follow through on those intentions? Why or why not? What happened as a result?

Continue your discussion of the Scripture passage using the following insights and questions:

From *Simon Peter*, by Adam Hamilton:

Jesus knew Peter's flaws. We have seen them, too, throughout the Gospel story. And so Jesus told him something that came to haunt him: "Truly I tell you, this very night, before the cock crows, you will deny me three times" (Matthew 26:34 NRSV). These must have been painful words for Peter to hear, being singled out by Jesus and told of his impending failure of nerve. He repeated his promise of loyalty: "Even though I must die with you, I will not deny you" (Matthew 26:35 NRSV).

- Why do you think Peter, who by this point had seen Jesus' wisdom and authority many times over, refused to believe Jesus' prediction that Peter would deny knowing him?
- According to Matthew (26:51), Mark (14:47), and Luke (22:50), when Jesus was arrested, someone with him cut off the high priest's slave's ear with a sword; John specifies the sword-swinger was Peter (18:10). Why did Jesus reject violent attempts to save him?
- Do you think Christians can or should ever use violence to stand up for someone else? If so, under what circumstances? If not, why not?

From *Simon Peter*, by Adam Hamilton:
While the Gospels don't contain all the same stories, this is the one story about Peter that all four Gospels record—his failure of nerve and his denial of Christ at Jesus' trial. Typically, following the death of revered figures, their shortcomings and failures are minimized, while their positive attributes and saintly stories are repeated and accentuated. So why would a church that loves Peter retell this story of Peter's denial?

I'm convinced that they told this story about Peter because Peter himself insisted on telling it over and over again. It became so associated with Peter and his ministry that not to tell the story would have been a great disservice.

- Why would Peter tell the early church about this incident? What does this story's presence in the Gospels suggest about their reliability?
- Do you have a story about your own shortcomings or failures that you tell others in the hopes that something good will come of it? How easy or hard is it for you to tell that story? Do you think others have learned valuable lessons from it? Why or why not?

From *Simon Peter*, by Adam Hamilton:

Peter's story is for all of us. Peter showed us that denying Jesus is part of our all-too-human experience as disciples.

But Peter's story also shows us that we need not be defined by our failures. God does not define us by the worst thing we ever did. Jesus makes amazing use of flawed disciples.

- When, if ever, have you experienced a moment like Peter did? What would you do or say differently if you could live that moment over? How has your memory of that moment shaped your witness as Jesus' follower in moments since?
- How does knowing God does not define us by our "worst thing ever" shape the way you define yourself—and the way you define other people? How is this idea good news for you?

Washing Feet and True Greatness

According to the Gospel of John, the meal Jesus and his disciples shared before his arrest was not a Passover seder (because the lambs for the Passover were being slaughtered at the same time Jesus was being crucified—see John 13:1; 19:14, 31). Instead, Jesus made an ordinary meal extraordinary by washing his disciples' feet.

From *Simon Peter*, by Adam Hamilton:

In assuming the role of a servant, Jesus was teaching once more. He attempted to help Peter and the disciples understand who he was, and what he demanded of them (and us).... The disciples would never forget this lesson.

For us, of course, the lesson isn't really about washing feet. That's not a routine task in our culture, although some churches still practice foot washing as a symbolic act. Jesus' lesson was much deeper, and once again Peter was the foil to let Jesus teach it. As Jesus put it in Luke's Gospel, "The greatest among you must become like a person of lower status and the leader like a servant" (Luke 22:26).

Discuss:

- What was so significant about Jesus' act of washing his disciples' feet? (See especially John 13:12-15, 34-35.)
- How does Peter's initial response to Jesus' act (John 13:6-9) show what he thought leadership should look like?
- How do you see people in your community and culture defining leadership and greatness? How does Jesus' example of washing feet confirm or challenge these ideas?
- What modern routine task would have the same impact as washing feet did in Jesus' society when performed for someone else?
- Talk about a time you have chosen to serve by focusing on someone else's needs rather than your own. What happened? Did that choice make you feel as though you had discovered more abundant living? Why or why not?
- Who is someone, known to you personally or not, you would point to as an example of "true greatness" as Jesus defines it? Why

Staring Straight at Jesus

In Luke's account of Peter's denial, the disciple's third protest that he doesn't know his rabbi may take place as Jesus is being led through the high priest's courtyard, because, "The Lord turned and looked straight at Peter" as the rooster crows (22:61). Jesus' direct gaze deepens Peter's sense of shame.

In some Christian traditions, believers worship with their direct gaze meeting Jesus' through the use of icons. Icons are religious artwork especially associated with the Eastern Orthodox Church. They are not painted (or "written") to be realistic depictions of biblical scenes and characters, but to be aids to prayer—almost "windows" through which the worshiper and Jesus can "see" each other.

Search the Internet or books of religious artwork for Eastern Orthodox icons depicting Jesus, perhaps in one of the biblical events described in chapter 4 of Adam Hamilton's book:

The Transfiguration
The Last Supper
Jesus washing the disciples' feet

Jesus' prayer and arrest in the garden of Gethsemane
Jesus' trial before Caiaphas

There is no single correct way to pray using an icon. Try this method or another of your choice:

- Display the icon where you can see it as you sit comfortably.
- Spend a minute or two letting your gaze roam freely over the icon.
- Notice the detail(s) that most consistently attracts your attention. Focus on that detail for a minute or two. Why do you think this part or parts of the icon stand out for you?
- If you try to imagine yourself with Jesus in this scene, what do you "see"?
- As you continue to gaze at the icon, what thoughts and feelings occur to you? Try not to "censor" yourself. You are seeking to be attentive to "nudgings" from the Holy Spirit. What situations, places, and people come to mind? How might the Spirit be leading you to incorporate these thoughts and feelings into your prayer?
- As you end your time of gazing at the icon, what response—perhaps an outward action, perhaps an internal commitment—do you sense Jesus calling you to make?

Closing Questions

Wrap up your session by discussing the following questions:

- What is one new insight or question you have after today's session about what it means to be recognized as Jesus' follower?
- What is one action you will take this week to publicly recognize Jesus?
- What is one way you will actively attend to others' interests before your own this week?

Closing Prayer

Use the following prayer or one of your own.

Dear Jesus, Teacher and Lord: Thank you for loving, saving, and transforming me. May I gladly proclaim you, through all I say and all I do, that others may also know your love and your abundant life. Amen.

5.

FROM COWARDICE TO COURAGE

Opening Activity: Wrap 'n' Run Relay Race

Supplies: masking tape, two jackets or coats

From *Simon Peter*, by Adam Hamilton:

Had the Crucifixion been the end of Jesus' story, it surely would have been the end of Peter's story too. Most likely he would have returned to Galilee and his fishing business. Or, if his life continued to be in danger from the religious leaders or the Romans, he may have fled to another country and assumed a new identity. Either way, chances are that Peter would have been lost to history.

We know, of course, that the cross wasn't the end of Peter's story, and that Peter went on to become the rock Jesus knew he could be. What happened to transform Peter, moving him from cowardice to unshakable courage?

Use masking tape to outline two "boats" on the floor. Put one jacket or coat in each "boat." An agreed distance away, mark a "beach" with the masking tape running the width of your playing space.

Form two teams of participants. Each team begins in one of the "boats." Before the race, read aloud John 21:7: "When Simon Peter heard it was the Lord, he wrapped his coat around himself (for he was naked) and jumped into the water." Explain that Peter may not have been fully clothed because too many garments might have interfered with his tossing of the fishing nets.

Tell teams that when the race begins, each team member must pick up the jacket, tie it around his or her waist, jump out of the "boat" and run to the "beach," then run back to the "boat," jump in, and unwrap the jacket from the waist and drop it for the next team member to pick up and repeat the process. The team in which all members complete the race first wins.

Opening Prayer

Use this prayer or one of your own:

Holy God, your Son Jesus' resurrection proves your victory over death and sin and sets us free to follow him with confidence. May we sense your Spirit's presence now through what we read, think, and say, that we may, like Simon Peter, greet our risen Lord with joy and commit ourselves to the work he calls us to do. Amen.

Read and Reflect on Scripture

As Adam Hamilton notes, "The Gospels record several different episodes when the resurrected Jesus appeared to his disciples." Each evangelist (Gospel writer) wanted to emphasize certain truths about and themes related to Jesus and so highlighted different traditions about when and how the risen Christ showed himself to his followers. But all agree he was raised, and he did appear.

The appearance recorded in John 21 takes place sometime after the first Easter morning:

Later, Jesus himself appeared again to his disciples at the Sea of Tiberias. This is how it happened: Simon Peter, Thomas (called Didymus), Nathanael from Cana in Galilee, Zebedee's sons, and two other disciples were together. Simon Peter told them, "I'm going fishing."

They said, "We'll go with you." They set out in a boat, but throughout the night they caught nothing. Early in the morning, Jesus stood on the shore, but the disciples didn't realize it was Jesus.

Jesus called to them, "Children, have you caught anything to eat?"

They answered him, "No."

He said, "Cast your net on the right side of the boat and you will find some."

So they did, and there were so many fish that they couldn't haul in the net. Then the disciple whom Jesus loved said to Peter, "It's the Lord!" When Simon Peter heard it was the Lord, he wrapped his coat around himself (for he was naked) and jumped into the water. The other disciples followed in the boat, dragging the net full of fish, for they weren't far from shore, only about one hundred yards.

When they landed, they saw a fire there, with fish on it, and some bread. Jesus said to them, "Bring some of the fish that you've just caught." Simon Peter got up and pulled the net to shore. It was full of large fish, one hundred fifty-three of them. Yet the net hadn't torn, even with so many fish. Jesus said to them, "Come and have breakfast." None of the disciples could bring themselves to ask him, "Who are you?" They knew it was the Lord. Jesus came, took the bread, and gave it to them. He did the same with the fish. This was now the third time Jesus appeared to his disciples after he was raised from the dead.

When they finished eating, Jesus asked Simon Peter, "Simon son of John, do you love me more than these?"

Simon replied, "Yes, Lord, you know I love you."

Jesus said to him, "Feed my lambs." Jesus asked a second time, "Simon son of John, do you love me?"

Simon replied, "Yes, Lord, you know I love you."

Jesus said to him, "Take care of my sheep." He asked a third time, "Simon son of John, do you love me?"

Peter was sad that Jesus asked him a third time, "Do you love me?" He replied, "Lord, you know everything; you know I love you."

Jesus said to him, "Feed my sheep. I assure you that when you were younger you tied your own belt and walked around wherever you wanted. When you grow old, you will stretch out your hands and another will tie your belt and lead you where you don't want to go." He said this to show the kind of death by which Peter would glorify God. After saying this, Jesus said to Peter, "Follow me."

—John 21:1-19

Discuss:

- What similarities and differences do you note when you compare this story to Luke 5:1-11, the first Scripture we read in this study of Simon Peter? What about the second Scripture we read, Matthew 14:22-33? How do these comparisons and contrasts help you understand this Scripture?
- Why do you imagine Peter and the other disciples have gone back to their former occupation of fishing after Jesus' resurrection?
- Given that this story occurs after Jesus' resurrection and the risen Jesus has already appeared twice in John's Gospel to most of the disciples (see 20:19-29), why do you think the disciples don't immediately recognize Jesus (21:4)?

Continue your discussion of the Scripture passage using the following insights and questions:

From *Simon Peter*, by Adam Hamilton:

Three times Simon denied Jesus. Three times Jesus asked for his love and loyalty, feeling Simon squirm a bit while wrestling with his denial. And three times Jesus reaffirmed his call for Simon to be the Rock upon which he would build his church.

- What words and actions in the story show us that Jesus is reaffirming Simon's call?

- Shared meals were an important part of Jesus' ministry before and after his resurrection. Read about some others: Mark 2:15-17; Luke 7:36-48; John 6:1-13; Matthew 26:26-30; Luke 24:28-32. Why do you think Jesus used meals as opportunities to teach and serve other people?
- What expectations might the disciples have brought to this surprise breakfast on the beach with the risen Jesus, given Jesus' past ministry through meals?
- What does the way Jesus used meals and food suggest about how Christians should view and use meals and food today?

From *Simon Peter*, by Adam Hamilton:

Adam Hamilton notes that John the evangelist's specific Greek word for the charcoal fire Jesus makes (verse 9)

> only occurs in one other place in the Gospels, in John 18:18 where Simon Peter is warming himself at a *charcoal* fire outside the high priest's house, while Jesus is on trial inside. It was at this fire that Simon Peter would deny knowing Jesus three times.

- Why do you think John so carefully draws a connection between these two charcoal fires? What is the larger significance, if any, of this small detail?
- Adam Hamilton also points out that Jesus twice asks Peter if Peter "loves" (Greek *agapao*—self-sacrificing love) him, to which Peter responds that he "loves" (Greek *phileo*—affectionate, brotherly love) Jesus. When Jesus asks Peter about loving him a third time, he asks, "Simon, do you *phileo* me?" Although Jesus and his disciples likely spoke Aramaic (similar to Hebrew), not Greek, John may be reflecting an actual change in Jesus' question. What do you think the change from *agapao* to *phileo* means? How could Peter's previous denial of Jesus help us understand the shift? Is one way of loving Jesus superior to the other, or does Jesus call for and welcome both?

- How do (or how should) Christians measure their love for Jesus? How do you?

From *Simon Peter*, by Adam Hamilton:

The way we express our love for Jesus is by caring for others. This might literally involve feeding them, as Jesus taught in the parable of the sheep and the goats: "I was hungry, and you gave me something to eat." It might involve meeting others' need for clothing or shelter. It might involve caring for them when they are sick or visiting someone in prison. What we do for others, Jesus says, is an expression of our love and devotion to him. In his interchange with Peter, Jesus boiled it down to a simple command: if you love me, then feed my sheep, and care for my lambs.

- How, specifically, are you answering Jesus' call to "feed his sheep" in your life?
- How is your youth ministry and congregation answering his call?

Science Experiment:

In the next chapter, Hamilton writes about the gift of the Holy Spirit at Pentecost (an event the evangelist Luke describes in Acts 2). Here's a simple science experiment to anticipate next week's lesson and help you illustrate and think about the Holy Spirit's power.

What You'll Need

empty plastic bottle (approximate size sixteen ounce)
latex balloon
plastic or ceramic bowl or container (big enough to set the bottle in)
hot water

What You'll Do

1. Remove the bottle's cap.
2. Fit the mouth of the balloon over the mouth of the bottle.
3. Pour hot water into the bowl (avoid heat-conducting metal bowls for your own safety).

4. Place the bottle into the hot water.
5. Observe what happens to the balloon.

The hot water heats the air inside the plastic bottle. This air rises because the heat causes its molecules to move faster and expand, which in turn causes the balloon to inflate.

In Acts 2, the Holy Spirit rushes upon the gathered believers like a warm and powerful wind. The Spirit's power caused Peter and the others to "move faster and expand"—to leave the upper room in Jerusalem and spread the good news about Jesus, ultimately, "to the end of the earth" (Acts 1:8).

Discuss:

- What other images do or could you use to visualize and think about the Holy Spirit's power?
- How has your youth ministry or congregation experienced the Spirit's power to make you "move faster and expand"?
- Do you agree with Adam Hamilton's statement that Christians today need the Spirit's power more than ever? Why or why not?

Lectio Divina

Lectio divina means "divine reading." It's an ancient Christian spiritual practice in which repeated, prayerful readings of the same Scripture passage become opportunities to sense the risen Christ's message for and call to us.

As with prayer using icons (in session 4), there's no single "right way" to do *lectio divina*. Here is one suggested method you can use with a portion of this session's Bible reading, John 21:6-17. If you are part of a group, recruit three different readers; if alone, read the text aloud yourself three times (or use an audio Bible or record yourself reading the text into a smartphone or other device, then listen three times).

First Reading: Listen for a word, phrase, or image from the text that "lights up" for you, that grabs your attention. After the reading, spend about one or two minutes silently contemplating that word, phrase, or image. What connections does it spark for you? How does it make you feel?

(If part of a group, after the silence, invite participants to share what attracted their attention. Do not ask follow-up questions or make comments at this point.)

Second Reading: During this reading, try to imagine yourself as present in the reading. What do you see? hear? touch? smell? taste? Does the same word or image "light up" for you during this reading, or another one? After the reading, spend about two or three minutes thinking about how this scene connects with your life today.

(If part of a group, after the silence, invite participants to comment briefly about how they saw themselves as a part of the scene in the text, or where they think the scene connects with their lives. Again, refrain from commenting or asking follow-up questions at this point.)

Third Reading: During the final reading, listen with this question in mind: *What is Jesus calling me to do, or who is Jesus calling me to be, through this text?* Spend about five minutes thinking and praying about this question.

(If part of a group, after the silence, invite participants to talk about their responses to the question. Other participants may now ask follow-up questions, but only to help the responder clarify what they sense Jesus is saying to them through the text, not to judge the responder's answer.)

Close the activity with a prayer of thanksgiving for Jesus' presence in the reading and hearing of Scripture.

Snack Suggestion: *Taiyaki*

To celebrate the risen Jesus' breakfast on the beach with his disciples, try making *taiyaki*, a fish-shaped pancake/waffle-like treat filled with a sweet red bean paste (although you could substitute other sweet fillings). You can find recipes online at such sites as http://eugeniekitchen.com/taiyaki/ or https://www.justonecookbook.com/taiyaki/. Special taiyaki pans are available for purchase online. (You could also consider toasting frozen round waffles, cutting them to look like fish, and making "sandwiches" with a sweet filling out of them—it wouldn't be authentic taiyaki, but it might be easier and faster depending upon what is available to you.)

As your group eats the snack, discuss ways you can organize or participate in efforts to feed people who are hungry, in obedience to Jesus' command to Peter.

Closing Questions

Wrap up your session by discussing the following questions:

- What is one new insight or question you have after today's session about what it means to express your love for Jesus?
- What is one way you will actively feed Jesus' sheep this week?

Closing Prayer

Use the following prayer or one of your own:

Risen Lord Jesus, because you live, we also will live. Give us courage to go where you lead and to feed other people with food and with your word and your love, in your holy name. Amen.

6.

THE REST OF THE STORY

Opening Activity:

Supplies: large assortment of objects, bedsheet

From *Simon Peter*, by Adam Hamilton:

In Acts 10:34-35 Peter says, "I really am learning that God doesn't show partiality to one group of people over another. Rather, in every nation, whoever worships him and does what is right is acceptable to him." This is a remarkable statement; Peter was still learning. His old views were changing. What he thought he knew about God and God's grace was being turned on its head. Even how he read and interpreted Scripture was changing in response to seeing God working in the lives of those he previously considered unclean.

I wonder if you ever have been surprised by God's grace. Have you been surprised to see God working in the lives of people you may not have expected?

Gather a large assortment of objects people can easily pick up and handle. The greater the number of unusual objects you can find, the better, but also include some common household items. Place a sheet in the middle of your meeting space and place all the objects on it.

As group members arrive, assign each one a number (assign numbers sequentially) and invite each person to choose an object from the sheet. Once all the objects are chosen, ask participants 1, 2, and 3 to put their objects back on the sheet. All group members should think of as many things as possible the objects have in common. The commonalities cannot be obvious (in other words, "They're all physical objects" isn't an acceptable answer). Encourage creativity and "out-of-the-box" thinking. When your group is done brainstorming commonalities for the first three objects, remove those objects and have participants 4, 5, and 6 place their objects in the sheet. Repeat the process until all objects have been put in the sheet.

Options: Work with groups of four or five objects, if appropriate for your group size. If gathering enough objects isn't practical, cut out pictures of objects from magazines and newspapers to use for the activity instead.

After the game, discuss:

- How easy or challenging was it to find things in common between the different objects?
- Did you find it easier to think of things uniting the objects the longer you played the game? Why or why not?
- What can this game tell us about discovering what different people have in common?

In the final session in our study of Simon Peter, we'll explore how he came to see a common bond where once he had seen only difference, as well as what his realization means for Jesus' followers today.

Opening Prayer

Use this prayer or one of your own:

Merciful God, you rule over all people and are at work, by your Spirit, to draw all people closer to yourself. Show us how you used Simon Peter to spread the good news of your love, and give us courage to tell others, as he did, about your welcoming embrace in Jesus Christ. Amen.

Read and Reflect on Scripture

From *Simon Peter*, by Adam Hamilton:

With the Spirit working through him, Peter was used by God to do amazing things—acts he had never done before, things he had only seen Jesus do.

Our final session in this study of Simon Peter's life highlights two stories from the Acts of the Apostles, which Luke the evangelist wrote as a sort of "sequel" to his Gospel (compare Luke 1:1-4 and Acts 1:1-2). Although we can figure out some of the early Christian church's history from the letters of Paul and others preserved in the New Testament, Acts is the only long narrative in the Bible about how Jesus' first followers spread the good news and started a movement (originally known as "The Way" [Acts 24:14]) that changed the world.

In the first story we'll read, we see how Peter did amazing things with the Holy Spirit working through him.

Peter and John were going up to the temple at three o'clock in the afternoon, the established prayer time. Meanwhile, a man crippled since birth was being carried in. Every day, people would place him at the temple gate known as the Beautiful Gate so he could ask for money from those entering the temple. When he saw Peter and John about to enter, he began to ask them for a gift. Peter and John stared at him. Peter said, "Look at us!" So the man gazed at them, expecting to receive something from them. Peter said, "I don't have any money, but I will give you what I do have. In the name of Jesus Christ the Nazarene, rise up and walk!" Then he grasped the man's right hand and raised him up. At once his feet and ankles became strong. Jumping up, he began to walk around. He entered the temple with them, walking, leaping, and praising God. All the people saw him walking and praising God. They recognized him as the same one who used to sit at the temple's Beautiful Gate asking for money.

They were filled with amazement and surprise at what had happened to him.

—*Acts 3:1-10*

Discuss:

- Why do you think Luke emphasizes the way the man and the apostles looked at each other? Why is it important for Jesus' followers to look at people whom others may tend not to see?
- What is it important for people not seen by society to see in Christians when they look at us?
- Read Isaiah 35. Isaiah is painting a picture of a future God will bring in which God's people and all creation experience healing and wholeness. How does Peter's healing of the man at the temple gate connect with Isaiah's prophecy and point to the same future?

Continue your discussion of the Scripture passage with the following insights and questions:

From *Simon Peter*, by Adam Hamilton:

We call stories like Peter's healing of Tabitha miracles because they are rare. They are not God's ordinary way of working in the world. God doesn't ordinarily suspend the biological and physiological laws by which our bodies operate solely because we've prayed and have faith. Because of this, it would be easy to conclude that miracles never happen. But the biblical stories, and my own experiences, lead me to think that, on occasion, for reasons I may never fully understand, God's Spirit and power bring about an unexpected result: a miracle.

- Do you believe healing miracles like the one Peter performed can or do still happen? Why or why not?
- What would you say to people who feel confused or angry because they have not received miracles like this one?
- How have you, or how has someone you know, experienced God's healing through another person? How, if ever, has someone else experienced God's healing through you?

- What makes Peter's gift to the man more valuable than money? How do you imagine this miracle affected the man's view of himself and his place in the community? How does it illustrate the kind of healing available to all people in Jesus?

This session's second story from Acts requires more setup. Remember that both Jesus and all his first followers were devout Jews. They obeyed the Law that God gave to Israel at Mount Sinai, a gift marking them as God's special people, chosen for service (see Exodus 19:5-6). Among other practices, the Law required all Jewish males be circumcised as sign of their membership in God's chosen people.

Jesus' ministry began among Jews before he ministered to Gentiles (non-Jews), and the early church may have assumed Jesus' church would remain Jewish. But while Peter was ministering in the towns of Lydda and Joppa—both well to the northwest of Jerusalem, a clue that Jesus' promise to his apostles in Acts 1:8 was already finding fulfillment—he experienced a vivid but confusing vision that called all such assumptions into question. When he returned to Jerusalem, he summarized his vision for the rest of the church, as well as what happened as a result of it and what he believed it all meant.

> The apostles and the brothers and sisters throughout Judea heard that even the Gentiles had welcomed God's word. When Peter went up to Jerusalem, the circumcised believers criticized him. They accused him, "You went into the home of the uncircumcised and ate with them!"

> Step-by-step, Peter explained what had happened. "I was in the city of Joppa praying when I had a visionary experience. In my vision, I saw something like a large linen sheet being lowered from heaven by its four corners. It came all the way down to me. As I stared at it, wondering what it was, I saw four-legged animals—including wild beasts—as well as reptiles and wild birds. I heard a voice say, 'Get up, Peter! Kill and eat!' I responded, 'Absolutely not, Lord! Nothing impure or unclean has ever entered my mouth.' The voice from heaven spoke a second time, 'Never consider unclean what God has made pure.' This happened three times, then everything was pulled back into heaven. At that moment three men who had been sent to me from Caesarea arrived at the house where we were

staying. The Spirit told me to go with them even though they were Gentiles. These six brothers also went with me, and we entered that man's house. He reported to us how he had seen an angel standing in his house and saying, 'Send to Joppa and summon Simon, who is known as Peter. He will tell you how you and your entire household can be saved.' When I began to speak, the Holy Spirit fell on them, just as the Spirit fell on us in the beginning. I remembered the Lord's words: 'John will baptize with water, but you will be baptized with the Holy Spirit.' If God gave them the same gift he gave us who believed in the Lord Jesus Christ, then who am I? Could I stand in God's way?"

Once the apostles and other believers heard this, they calmed down. They praised God and concluded, "So then God has enabled Gentiles to change their hearts and lives so that they might have new life."

—Acts 11:1-18

Discuss:

- Why was entering the house of Cornelius, a Roman centurion, such an unusual thing for Peter to have done? Why did it upset Peter's fellow believers in Jerusalem? (For help, read Acts 10:28-29.)
- In his vision, why doesn't Peter want to kill and eat the animals in the sheet, as the heavenly voice tells him to? What truth finally answers Peter's objections? How would you put that truth in your own words?
- What connections does Peter make between his vision and the Spirit's summons to go with the Gentiles who came looking for him? How does what Peter sees the Spirit do when he goes with the Gentiles convince him he understood his vision correctly?
- What does Peter's experience lead the rest of the church in Jerusalem to realize?
- How have you seen God at work in surprising people? How has what you've seen challenged your old ideas about who's in and who's out?

- Talk about a time when you were surprised to realize how big God is. What prompted your realization, and what did you do or are you still doing about it?
- How have you tried to share your experience of God's greatness with others, as Peter shared his?

Uncontainable Excitement for Christ!

Once, when ordered by the religious authorities to stop preaching about Jesus, Peter and John replied, "As for us, we can't stop speaking about what we have seen and heard" (Acts 4:20).

> ### From *Simon Peter*, by Adam Hamilton:
> That's how Peter and the apostles have felt about Jesus' impact on their lives. It was so profound that Peter had to share it. He couldn't stop talking about it. Has your faith impacted you in this way? Has your experience with the risen Christ been so life-giving that you had to share it? Have you been so filled by the Spirit that you just had to tell others about your faith in Christ?

Hamilton goes on to compare Peter and the other believers talking about Jesus to grandparents who have to tell others about their grandkids because the excitement just "spills out." (Do you have grandparents or other adults who brag on you? Then you know what Adam Hamilton is talking about!)

You may already be familiar with the "Mentos and Coke" science demonstration. If you're not, you can easily find videos of it online, as well as instructions on how to perform it yourself (such as "Spurting Science" from Scientific American, https://www.scientificamerican.com/article/bring-science-home-coke-mentos/). Here are the basics: take a roll of Mentos candy and a bottle of carbonated soda to a large, open space where you can safely make a mess, drop the candy into the soda, and stand back!

When the candies break the bonds between the carbon dioxide and the water in the soda, they create a physical reaction that the soda bottle just can't contain. And when Jesus Christ breaks our bondage to sin, evil, and death, we shouldn't be able to contain our excitement any more than Peter could.

Discuss:

- How do you answer these questions from Adam Hamilton: "Has your experience with the risen Christ been so life-giving that you had to share it? Have you been so filled by the Spirit that you just had to pass it on?"
- When was a time you felt very excited about sharing your faith in Christ? What did you do?
- How do you share your faith when you don't feel excited about doing so?
- Does being excited by your experience with Jesus always mean sharing your faith in exciting ways? Why or why not?

Closing Questions

Wrap up your session by discussing the following questions:

- What is one new insight or question you have after today's session about the reach of God's grace?
- What is one way you will actively share your experience with Jesus with other people this week?
- As we close our study of Simon Peter, what will you remember most about "the prince of the apostles" and why?
- If Peter were to say one thing to encourage you in your faith, what do you think he would say? What do you think he would say to encourage your youth ministry or congregation in its continued witness to Jesus?

Closing Prayer

Use this prayer or one of your own:

We thank and praise you, O God, for the life and the legacy of your servant, Simon Peter. We are grateful for the times he showed us what living as a bold follower of Jesus looks like, and we are grateful for the times he showed us that your faithfulness to sinners never fails. By your Holy Spirit, may we trust your love and your power, as he did, and may we always proclaim to others, in word and in action, that your Son is the Savior. Amen.

NOTES

1. Inspired by Katherine Bilsborough, "Katherine Bilsborough: A Simple Idea—The Weekend Game," TeachingEnglish, https://www.teachingenglish.org.uk/blogs/katherine-bilsborough/katherine-bilsborough-a-simple-idea-weekend-game.

2. Based on "Science Project: Water Pressure at Depth," Education.com, https://www.education.com/science-fair/article/earth-science_squirter1/.

3. Adapted from "Sink or Swim (Surface Tension)—SICK Science," Steve Spangler Science, https://www.stevespanglerscience.com/lab/experiments/sink-or-swim-surface-tension/.

4. Andrew Zimmerman Jones, "Surface Tension—Definition and Experiments," ThoughtCo, updated March 31, 2018, https://www.thoughtco.com/surface-tension-definition-and-experiments-2699204.

5. Adapted from "Sinkholes in a Cup," Earth Science Week, http://www.earthsciweek.org/classroom-activities/sinkholes-cup, and Clay Ostarly, "Sinkhole Science: A Simple Experiment," YouTube, January 13, 2015, https://www.youtube.com/watch?v=HPEo9iL65gA.

6. Adapted from Melissa (blogger), "Making a Cross Necklace Out of Nails—Kid Friendly Things To Do .com," Kid Friendly Things to Do, https://kidfriendly thingstodo.com/2016/03/making-a-cross-necklace-out-of-nails-kid-friendly -things-to-do-com/.

7. "A Covenant Prayer in the Wesleyan Tradition," in *The United Methodist Hymnal* (Nashville: The United Methodist Publishing House, 1989), 607.

Made in the USA
Monee, IL
01 June 2023